Disability Matters

Source: A man diagnosed as suffering from acute dementia. Lithograph, 1892, after a drawing by Alexander Johnston. Wellcome Collection

<hr>

Disability Matters

Carol Beardmore, Steven King and Geoff Monks

CALL OF CROWS

2018

First published in Great Britain in 2018
by Call of Crows
Rutland

Printed and bound by Lulu
Cover and text design by Carol Beardmore
Cover image: Processing language, left brain hemisphere
Wellcome Collection

ISBN: 978-1-912523-01-6

CALL OF CROWS

Contents

Acknowledgements

This book arises out of a grant from the Teaching Development Fund of the College of Social Sciences, Arts and Humanities, University of Leicester. We are grateful to the Committee for this funding. The central purpose of the grant was to explore, with a group of undergraduate and postgraduate students, the sense that 'history matters' when we come to look at current issues around mental and physical impairment and the constructions of these impairments into disability or degrees of ability. After many years of teaching 'disability history', we had come to realise that whether we focus on socio-medical constructions of disability, broadly conceived 'disability benefits', othering, or the cultural assimilation of physical difference, the degree of path dependency is often profound. Our students saw this too, and so our grant application was made in partnership with a group of them. The joint intent was to undertake two pieces of work. The first was a series of five audio podcasts in which we would explore the historical roots of modern policy dilemmas, consciously seeking out the voices of those with mental or physical impairments from historical documents to look at matters of continuity and change. These podcasts, recorded in the voices of the students themselves, are now available on Youtube. This book, loosely based upon the scripts for those podcasts (themselves variously authored by Carol Beardmore and Steve King), is the second of the outputs. Here, in this slightly more 'academic' forum, we seek to illustrate the absolute imperative for modern policy makers, pressure groups and think tanks to understand the essential history of disability.

Our group of undergraduate and postgraduate students have originated the podcast series and we are grateful to them for ideas that came out of the making of those podcasts, some of which now feature here: Janet Couloute, Cara Dobbing, Elizabeth Round, and Hamdan Mansoor. Roger Dickinson as Academic Director for the College of Social Sciences, Arts and Humanities has encouraged the project and we are grateful to him. More widely, we thank the six cohorts of undergraduate students who have at some point 'done disability' with us; the teaching of them has melded fundamentally into the text which follows.

Carol Beardmore, Steve King and Geoff Monks, April 2018.

Chapter 1: Constructing Disability

Thank you for buying our book on 'Disability Matters', which is underpinned by three broad aims. Firstly, we want to explore the historical roots of modern questions about how communities, stakeholder groups and policy-makers do and should think about people who have mental and physical impairments. In particular, we are interested in how medical, social and welfare policies in relation to such impairments have developed over the last thirty years, and some of the dilemmas, particularly in the area of welfare policy, that now resonate across the socio-political spectrum. Many of these will be familiar to you: how to deal with the rapidly increasing numbers of those with the physical and mental impairments that emerge out of extreme old age; whether and how to define those with physical impairments as 'able' and thus to oblige them to find work; how to deal with funding shortfalls in the NHS as it struggles and fails to meet the spiralling costs of intervening in areas of mental and physical impairment; and questions over what the proper balance between state, voluntary and private actions should be on these and other issues. Modern policy-makers, fund-holders, charities and even disability pressure groups construct these questions as essentially 'new'. In fact, they are not. To take just one example, the Victorian State and its people worried incessantly that charities and the local authorities which were in charge of paying for welfare were being deceived by the idle and disorderly who dressed their laziness up in the clothes of physical impairment (King 2015; Borsay 2005). Such worries look little different to the modern obsession with potential fraud that led to recent attempts to tighten eligibility for getting and retaining disability living allowances. Exploring the historic roots of present dilemmas is thus in itself a useful corrective to shallow thinking about mental and physical impairment.

Our second aim relates to this point, which is to say that policy-makers, politicians, fund-holders, charities and pressure groups all work with a common narrative that somehow things have 'got better' over time for those with mental and physical impairments, at least compared to the distant past. The modern dilemmas thrown up, for instance, by a rapidly ageing population are constructed almost uniformly in terms of protecting or consolidating the gains of the last

30 years even if simultaneously containing costs. Applying the gaze of an historian offers a different perspective. The question of what to 'do' with an increasingly old and sick life-cycle group was as much a reality in the later nineteenth-century as it is now. The tenor of public debate about the issue, and wider matters of inter-generational fairness, feels much the same as it did in the 1880s and 1890s when Governments across Europe were beginning to formulate the idea of the State Pension (Thane 2000; Hennock 2007). More widely, we might argue that 'history matters' because the way in which past societies have confronted dilemmas which we see as modern points to solutions which do not currently sit on the policy-making table. To take just one example, an historian might ask of the current debate about how far we can cut the costs of disability benefits: is it better to have a legal right to welfare as now, or a moral right, as in the past. Legal rights can be (and are being) watered down. Moral rights are rather harder to dislodge. In turn, a conversation about moral rights (much as happened in the nineteenth-century) moves attention away from the condition and treatment of the individual and towards the responsibility of the social systems in which they live, creating a rather different potential policy landscape. Asking a question like this – an historian's question – speaks to a wider canvas of public debate about the construction and deconstruction of impairment outside of Westminster, think tanks and campaigning groups.

A third aim, then, is to bring the skills of the historian to an understanding of the process by which mental and physical impairment is (and has been) constructed into narratives of disability (Borsay 2005; Turner 2012; Suzuki 2006). That disability is a socially and medically constructed label applied to ordinary people by those with power, is now well accepted. But this narrative is insufficient. Disability as a category has been constructed and reconstructed continually, often with the active or covert support of those living with impairments and losing sight of this fact makes for feeble debate about how society does and ought to think about such people. Throughout this volume, you will thus see that history really does matter.

To explore these issues, we will use historical material throwing light on a suite of mental and physical impairments. Our focus will be on the nineteenth-century, the period before disability legislation and defined disability benefits took hold. This approach is deliberate. Our underlying thought has been to locate the roots of modern policy dilemmas in the period immediately before 'policy' is formed but also in an age that looks in terms of problems such as ageing populations, the incidence of blindness and the level of physical incapacity, much like our own. Uniquely in recent debate, we will concentrate our analysis largely on the words and voices of those with mental and physical impairments, and within this envelope on the words and experiences of ordinary people rather than the educated or the noisy activists. We will look at how ordinary people understood their impairments and how they exercised agency and voice to try and shape the way that they were perceived, constructed and treated. In the process we will show that 'modern' questions (such as whether we should think and talk in terms of disability or instead of various degrees of *ability*) have distinct historical roots.

Our volume is timely. On some measures, Britain is now the 'most disabled' country in Europe. The proportion of the population on some form of 'disability welfare' is by some distance the highest in Europe. Policy responses have included *inter alia* persistent attempts by all political parties to water down the level of, and entitlement to, disability benefits; the construction of a narrative of the need for those with mental and physical impairments to get back into work as a good in itself; and the rationing of NHS resources, particularly in areas such as mental health. These current issues are important. In the sense that they are path dependent a group of historians can and should bring important new perspectives to bear. Yet, compared to the problems coming down the tracks, our current dilemmas will seem like a walk in the park. A rapidly ageing population threatens an epidemic of mental and physical impairment. As James Riley has argued for the nineteenth-century, those living longer tend also to live sicker (Riley 1997). An epidemic of obesity and associated conditions such as diabetes will drive a surge in amputations, lost sight and physical incapacity. The so-called 'snowflake' generation of people under the age of 30 appear to have mental health problems on a scale not seen in the modern era. Sight problems relating to screen use, poor nutrition and ageing are once more surging, reaching levels not seen since the Industrial Revolution. We could go on, but the point is that new policy solutions will be needed. Tinkering or doing nothing, seemingly the modus operandi of all political parties, will not be sustainable. Our contention is that looking at how past societies have dealt with similar problems can point us to different policy futures. In the chapters that follow we thus focus on the history of sensory impairment (blindness, deafness), physical impairment and mental health, with each chapter driven by one or more current policy dilemmas. Treating such impairments as discrete is not of course correct – either historically or currently – given the inter-correlation of conditions at the individual level, but this wider issue may be the subject of our future work with students at Leicester University, De Montfort University and the Open University.

Chapter 2 Blindness and Visual Impairment

In the last chapter we dealt (on the broadest canvas) with the ways in which an understanding of 'the past' of mental and physical impairment might inform current debates and future policy. To develop this theme and capitalise on the rich historical documentation that can throw light on sensory impairment, we move on in this chapter to the issue of lost and compromised sight. One particularly rich source for this sort of analysis is the pauper letter. Between 1601 and the 1660s the State developed, for England and Wales, a welfare system which focused in terms of decision-making and tax raising powers on the ecclesiastical parish. At the heart of that system were four principles which, with various tweaks, were to persist until the inter-war years of the twentieth-century: that poverty should be assessed and relieved at the local level by people who could have some intimate knowledge of the individuals making claims on the parish and by extension the State; that those falling into poverty for whatever reason should have a right to apply for welfare payments at a single place where they had settlement, that is a legally defined 'belonging'; that only the most deserving of these applicants should get welfare, though the State defined neither a list of those who should be deemed deserving nor set down how those people thus defined should be treated; and that those turned down for welfare should have (at least up until 1834) a right of appeal to external arbitration (Snell 2006; King 2000; Hindle 2004).

For those who did not migrate away from their place of belonging, falling into poverty or the threat of it would involve a call on a local official or attendance at a meeting of the ratepayers (the modern equivalent would be Council Tax payers) who met the bills for local welfare. We find the outcomes of such interactions in the annual accounts of the overseer of the poor or in the minutes of ratepayer meetings (so-called vestries or select vestries), sometimes with the colourful detail which allows us to understand the experiences of those receiving welfare and the sentiments of those who granted it. For another group, and one growing rapidly in terms of absolute numbers and percentage of the population by 1800, the issue of how to apply for welfare was rather more problematic. These were the people who had moved on from their place of belonging, sometimes only across the shortest of distances but often to rather more far-flung communities. Some of these people might have been 'away' for decades or indeed most of a lifetime, but they still had the right to apply for welfare only in the place where they belonged. In such cases the poor or prospectively poor person might return 'home' either to live or to make an application in person. Much more likely, they would write a letter of appeal or get someone else to write on their behalf, often dictating the contents of the letter eventually sent. On receipt, parochial officials might act as requested, modify their response according to their perception of the condition of the pauper or the scale of their local resources, seek further information, reject the appeal or just ignore it and hope not to receive another. Where welfare was granted, it might be with strings (the poor person could be forced to quit their host community and come 'home' or they could be subject to regular inspection) or rather more open-ended. Payments could be in cash, kind or via a third party in the host community (King 2005).

The existence of such pauper letters (and the associated letters of advocates and writers for the poor and the correspondence of officials who had to deal with the claims) has been known since the 1980s (Taylor 1989), but it was not until the late 1990s or early 2000s, and particularly in the work of Thomas Sokoll on collections in Essex, that historians began to appreciate the value of this nexus of correspondence for understanding of the voices and experiences of the most ordinary people, including many with mental and physical impairments (Hitchcock, King and Sharpe 1997; Sokoll 1997, 2000 and 2001). Subsequent work by historians of welfare, gender, disability and class has revealed that the letters identified in the 1990s and early 2000s were merely the tip of the iceberg in terms of surviving sources and that, additionally, many more letters were sent and can be traced as having been sent, than have in fact survived (Jones 2015). We now know that they constitute the largest single source available to study ordinary people and that the sense of limited literacy that has dominated prior understanding of the period from the late eighteenth to mid-nineteenth centuries must be substantially revised. These letters are not, of course, without their problems: are the ones that survive representative of all of those originally sent? Did the person signing the letter really write it? Where someone just marked the letter with an 'X' by way of signature because they could not write, should we regard the letters, sentiments and experiences set out in the prior letter as 'theirs'? Can and should letters be read out of context from the correspondence of officials and advocates which relate to them? Did writers tell the truth or did they embellish and lie? Do the sentiments, words and experiences of those who were 'out of place' and thus had to write adequately reflect the words, sentiments and experiences of those who remained in their place of belonging and thus dealt with local officials face-to-face? (King 2015b; King 2016). These issues have been explored at length by historians of welfare, but Thomas Sokoll ultimately concludes that the text of these letters provide us with a genuine, truthful and representative window onto the words and lives of the poor (Sokoll 2001). We follow this viewpoint and thus make extensive use of letters in the chapters that follow. We ask you to implicitly accept the argument that such material provides the only credible and large-scale way to understand the experiences of those with mental and physical impairment (most of whom did <u>not</u> end up in institutional contexts and thus within the records kept by such institutions) before the late twentieth-century. Here, in the epistolary nexus of the parish, the words and agency of those with impairments emerge. Through them we can trace the nuances of the socio-cultural construction of disability first touched upon in chapter one.

Against this backdrop, we begin this analysis of the value of historical perspective for current debates about visual impairment with the words of Mary Gunnell, sent in a letter to her 'home' parish of Great Oxendon (Leicestershire) from Manchester on 22 January 1834:

> Gentlemen
>
> About a fortnight ago my late husband wrote to you stating his and our Situation saying that he expected it would be his last time of troubling you which has been the case he Departed this transitory life on last Monday but one. We have not as yet received your answer I therefore write to inform you that I am left in a very precarious Situation as our Landlady has taken part of our Goods and I am in other Cases much embarrassed and in Respect to myself I am very Poorly in health and the worst is the loss of sight. I have long lost the sight of one Eye totally and have a Pearl

far advancing upon the other. You will consider I am not able to provide for myself. Daughter Elizabeth is still at home but it is not in her power to support me but is willing to do her utmost if you will assist her I therefore hope you will have the Goodness to take our Situation into consideration and favour me with an immediate Answer as I must have assistance from some Quarter

Gunnell described her predicament in graphic terms, pointing to the recent death of her husband, a landlady who had taken up and sold part of her household goods to pay for rent arrears, and her despair at not being able to make do even with the help of a daughter who still lived at home. Yet Gunnell's greatest fear was losing her sight. Already blind in one eye, she had 'a Pearl' – we would now understand this as a cataract – slowly depriving her of sight in the remaining eye. This, she worried, would compromise her long-term independence of the State, but she held out to the reader of the letter the possibility that if helped now in timely fashion she might be able to put off dependence for some time. This sense that investment now would serve the purpose of reducing future bills is a familiar strategy in pauper letters (King and Jones 2016). It also has sustained resonance with modern arguments in favour of maintaining eligibility for Disability Living Allowance, where early intervention is often seen as a way of saving the State money in the long–term.

For a modern population, cataracts have become at worst a minor irritation, surgically correctible in a process with low failure rates. The development of medical solutions to other aspects of modern blindness (from birth, through accident, or accumulating over a lifetime) has, however, been rather less spectacular. Stem cells, implants and transplants continue to promise much, but we are some way off anything that might be transformational for a wide cross-section of the population. At the same time, degenerative eye conditions are increasing in both volume and intensity, so that the future is not just an ageing population but an increasingly un- or poorly-sighted one. Just as Mary Gunnell could not simply have her cataract 'seen to' – safer eye surgery does not really begin to develop until the twentieth-century (Stanley 2003) – so the modern aged will have to manage their conditions rather than cure them. For individuals, society as a whole, and for politicians and social-welfare systems, this situation poses very real dilemmas over the nature and scope of care, appropriate welfare packages, individual versus collective responsibility for reducing eye problems and coping with their consequences, and about the role of families in supporting those with poor and deteriorating sight. Some recent commentators have been very much alive to these issues. To an historian, however, the striking thing about such 'modern' dilemmas is how they were very much shared by individual, families and policy-makers in the nineteenth-century, the last 'age' in which blindness and deteriorating sight simply had to be managed rather than cured (Phillips 2004). The questions of how such historical actors experienced, confronted and constructed visual impairment can thus potentially reveal important lessons for modern commentators.

As a starting point, it is important to remember that we have a very imperfect understanding of the scale and intensity of sight problems in the past. Oddly, the modern statistics on this matter are hardly any better than the historical ones. The late nineteenth-century census asked people to record whether a member of the family was blind, but it did not define what blindness meant. Did having one eye, for instance, count as blindness? When did the blurred vision associated with progressive cataracts spill over into 'blindness'? Because individual householders were free to interpret the label much as they wished, the census figures really tell us very little (Levitan 2011). What we *can* say is that the range of conditions or experiences leading to blindness, partial sight or deteriorating sight *was* extraordinarily common. As well as blindness from birth, compromised vision was created by workplace environments, industrial and agricultural accidents, the consequences of diseases such as smallpox, other infections, cataracts, ageing and war. It is these issues that we explore here. Let us first return to the issue of cataracts. Mary Gunnell was by no means uncommon in her experience of this problem, as the words of Thomas Weld, written to his home parish of Lyndhurst (Hampshire) from Guildford in Surrey on 19 August 1831, show:

> Sir, You well Know that I am almost blind through a Pearl
> on my Eye and I must ask a little assistance of you My
> business is of a cabinet maker and the finer sort and if I
> cannot See so I must Not work and my wages must be

reduced To a Meer Trickle through rough work on the piece or from neighbours Think Sir how you Might Feel if wrought to this end and not able as a man of the family to keep your Own Children from Starving and Nakedness and then you must surely Offer help to your poor petitioner, a trifle per week would allow me some Rest that might do me some good and some medicall aid might do the Job and would be Remembered with such Gratitude by Your Humble Servt Thomas Weld.

For Weld, the cataract on his left eye represented a threat to his work as a cabinet maker, one which promised to plunge his family into penury. Given this was highly skilled work, Weld's very identity as a man and head of household was threatened and he now asked his parish both for financial support (he felt that a period of rest would do him good) and unspecified medical help. Weld was comparatively young to be experiencing cataracts and the parish officers to whom he wrote clearly saw the threat of a lifetime of dependency for both him and his family. They quickly referred him to a doctor, who then charged them for assorted visits, 'drops' and ointments, and paid for an extended visit to Bath to take the waters, which they hoped would 'do him some good'. In fact, and something recorded in subsequent letters, Weld's sight was to deteriorate further up until we lose track of him in 1834.

The responsiveness of the State in the guise of parochial officers is striking and, particularly for the young or middle aged, usually duplicated across the more than 200 letters at our disposal that refer to or imply the existence of cataracts. At no point, however, did the authorities construct or label Weld as disabled. Rather, and in common with Weld himself, they calibrated their medical and financial responses to his deteriorating condition and sought to enhance and exploit his remaining *ability*. When Weld wrote in 1834 that he 'could not do as before' but that he might still get work in 'common joinery' and thus 'do for my family with but limited surport' he thus offered a partnership between State and individual brokered on the basis of capacity and not incapacity. Readers who know anything about modern disability benefit tests will recognise this bargain as essentially 'modern'. Perhaps more accurately, we can see that the modern response is really just a return to historical practice; it is just that politicians, claimants, policy-makers and civil servants do not realise this to be the case.

It is impossible to understand the exact extent and impact of cataracts because historically the condition merges seamlessly with other sight problems which present in old age. Nonetheless, macular degeneration appears with extraordinary regularity in our corpus of letters. David and Martha Clarke, were resident in Norwich but wrote seeking welfare support to their home parish of Peterborough in February 1801:

> Gentlemen
> I am sorry the distress of the times forces me to implore your immediate assistance I need not point out the dearness of articles of life flattering myself I write to gentlemen well aquainted with every circumstance of the kind and whome I trust are Gentlemen Ridy to redress your porre parishoners real distresses haveing laboured under depravity of site for several years and my wife under a very bad state of health and now at this time being bad In this Distrest situation I am force contrary to my wishes to ask your relief being quite unable to get through life I have no family that can come charge surety to you but hour selves but the frequent whant of work and the state of health we now labour under forcess your perishoners than to address you
> We are with submission
> Your humble servants

As with so many elderly writers, lost or failing sight was just one of a wider suite of problems which informed appeals for assistance. In this case inflation, unemployment and the illness of Martha Clarke, exacerbated an already dire situation and necessitated a plea for 'immediate assistance'.

Readers will be acutely aware of the resonance between 1801 and the present, when those in advanced old age are frequently labelled 'complex' cases. The resonances do not, however, end here. The letter contends that the Clarke's are quite alone – they have no family to come and help them or enter into partnership with the parish authorities – and that this too pushes them to an urgent appeal for communal assistance. The officials who received this letter and considered its distinctly modern dilemmas did not seek to send David Clarke to a doctor or medical institution to try and cure his 'depravity of site'. Clarke himself did not request such aid. Both parties accepted that failing sight and old age went hand-in-hand, much as we seek to 'manage' macular degeneration today. Rather, the State – in the guise of parish authorities – sought partnership with the couple, seeking to provide them with financial assistance to prevent complete destitution on the basis that the Clarke's would help themselves by taking whatever work opportunities or chances for economy that might come their way. Again, there is no sense – in practice or rhetoric – that the Clarke's saw themselves as anything other than less able than had previously been the case. While the word disability, with many of its modern connotations, was well established in the linguistic register by the time the Clarke's wrote (Turner 2012), it was not used in this case nor more widely for other writers with age-related sight problems.

The situation for another group with compromised sight – those who experienced industrial, agricultural, transport or domestic accidents or were blinded by violence or in the armed services – is more complex. Such people became more and more common in British society in the aftermath of the Napoleonic wars of the early nineteenth-century, with the rise of mechanised industrial and agricultural production, and the proliferation of urban living. Edward Edwards, the vicar of Huntingdon, wrote to Joseph Yates's home parish of Peterborough on his behalf on 12 July 1803 given that blindness prevented Yates himself from either attending the parish or addressing the officials direct:

> Joseph Yates, Glover & Breeches maker … is a quite, inoffensive, industrious man in the 69th year of his age His sight has been taken through a fire at his place of work some 6 years since that has left him all but blind and his earnings are consequently diminished considerably He therefore humbly submits his case to your consideration and hopes that you will allow him some weekly assistance. It is some reluctance that he make this application, having always endeavoured to avoid being beholden to Parish relief. A small sum weekly will satisfy him.

After the fire that took his sight, Yates had found some way to carry on his trade, or a version of it, notwithstanding his blindness. Now, six years after the event, his earnings proved insufficient and he applied, in effect, for what we would understand in a modern sense as 'in work benefits'. The parish responded as requested, though whether out of compassion, fear of higher bills if they did not act promptly, or because Yates had managed to get a man of high social status to write on his behalf, is unclear (King and Jones 2016). Whatever the reason, neither Yates nor parish officials viewed the case as one of disability. Carrying on the trade of glover and breeches maker at any level when blind is no mean feat and the fact of it points to a distinctly modern sense in which a close association between physical impairment and work opportunities can upset some of the negative connotations of the word 'disability'.

On the other hand, certain work accidents *do* seem to have attracted use of the term. Philip Jenkins, a boiler tender at a factory in Birmingham was blinded when his steam engine blew up in December 1828. This and associated blast injuries led the advocate who wrote for him to say that Jenkins was 'quite disabled from anything on his own account' and to ask the parish for a regular pension. Similarly, James Sneath was blinded by splinters when his workshop collapsed in Derby in June 1824. This and associated crush injuries and fracture of the skull led the parish officer to write to Mary Wild, Sneath's daughter and note that 'knowing of your father's depravity of site and this not the least of his problems, we will grant you 4s weekly and this you must endevor to supplement as best you can'. The exact combination of accident consequences that led to people accruing the label 'disabled' is unclear, but certainly the loss or impairment of sight itself was not a sufficient condition for this to happen.

A less familiar cause of blindness and failing sight – that associated with poor diet or diseases – also occasioned varying responses from the local State. Smallpox in particular has significance here. The disease was diminishing in importance by the early nineteenth-century, a function of both a decline in natural virulence and the impact of inoculation and later vaccination (Bennett 2012; Razzell 1977; Williams 2011). Nonetheless, its legacy was felt in accumulated life histories of blind eyes, pockmarked faces, compromised lungs and stunted growth. And even in the 1830s smallpox epidemics were both frequent and carried significant health consequences at the individual level (Shuttleton 2007). We come across disease-related blindness surprisingly often in our letters from or about the sick poor, as the words of Mary Young, written by her (as is obvious from the nature of the text) in March 1819, show:

> Gentlemen I must wreite to you with the most umble rerquest that you help me in my gratist hour of need I am Mary Young, Daur of Wm Young that lived in the Priory Field with him and I have maid doo as much as I could without cuming to you Sirs by selling littel things from my Baskitt that I can pick up or bye and for so maney years I have kept myself respecerable even thow I can see but littel since I was a gurl and now that my eyes go into night forevur I cannot make do no longur and so Sir with no wun to turn to I ask my parish to stand my frend at this last bit of inderpeindence for I am all alone and derpendint pon my naybers and frends for those little everyday things that have kept me from your door

Aged around 38, Young had been blind in one eye and had failing sight in the other since suffering from smallpox at age nine. Never married, she had lived with her parents until their death and had made a contribution to their household economy by selling goods on the street 'from my baskitt' (King 2004). This occupation – regarded at the time as a cross between begging and entrepreneurship (Althammer 2007) – had kept her 'respectable' but now, as her sight finally failed and with 'no wun [that is, a husband] to pretect me', she applied to her parish because she was 'all alone and derpendint pon my naybers and frends for those little everyday things' that kept her independent. Neither Young nor her parish regarded the lost sight as absolutely disabling, but the case has extensive resonance with modern concerns, embodied in terms such as 'the big society', about engendering a new sense of neighbourliness and community action to support the aged and sick.

Other diseases too had strong potential to remove or reduce sight, notably tuberculosis, which was endemic in nineteenth-century British society. The words of Thomas Hall, resident of Bristol, who wrote 'home' to his parish on 19 February 1817, exemplify this situation:

> Gentlemen I flatter myself that I talk to Gentlmn who know my case and will be willing to show some Christian feeling towards a poor parishioner I have been in Decline some time and have not had the breathe in my Body to work and always coughing the blood so that I barely have any left in me and the doctor holds no hope for my recovery and the worst is That now I lose my sight so that I cannot see from my Window as I stand confined to my bed and at elbows with the world I do not want to be troubling you and hope to do a little towards my Subsistence but a poor blind man must have your aid.

Hall's described symptoms included coughing blood, heaviness of breathing, infirmity and (the true test of the severity of illness in nineteenth-century England) confinement to bed and withdrawal from society (Porter and Porter 1988). However, one major additional side-effect of tuberculosis was a decline of sight progressing week-by-week to inevitable blindness. While Hall hoped eventually to be well and able to 'do a little' towards his subsistence, he asked the parish officers to enter into partnership with his family (in the form of a married son) so that he might maintain a semblance of independence. The request, and parochial assent to the arrangement, would have a distinctively 'modern' feel for readers with detailed knowledge of hospital bed-blocking and care in the community.

How parishes should deal with those who were blind from birth rather than becoming so over a life-cycle, was less clear to officials (Phillips 2004). In terms of official definitions of 'deservingness' for welfare benefits blind children who then turned into blind adults were near the very top of the list for both parochial support and additional personal philanthropy from the middling sorts and wealthy (Borsay 2012). On the other hand, from the sixteenth-century onwards English society periodically worried about wandering vagrants and beggars much as we do today. Those pretending to be blind formed, in the minds of critics of philanthropy and State welfare, a particular sub-group because any charlatan could fake blindness (Dyson and King 2007). It is no doubt for this reason that those blind from birth went to extra lengths to set out their efforts to be independent when they wrote to their home parishes, as the case of Elizabeth Brown (in a letter written on her behalf by her landlord Sally Webster of Gosport to Brown's home parish of Lyndhurst in January 1833 shows:

> Honored Sir, I am urged by the distress and suffering that I indure to state to you that I cannot avoid soliciting some additional assistance at this time of the Year as my Eyes are dreadfully inflamed so that I am totally blind and otherwise ill and lame that I can Gentlemen to grant me some extra relief

Brown followed this letter up with a more detailed missive (in a different hand, which may have been her own), one month later:

> Worthy Sir, I hope you will have the goodness to excuse my taking the liberty of requesting you, to represent to the Gentlemen of your Parish, my distressed situation, and inability to exert myself to any advantage, which compels me to throw myself on their generosity for an encreased allowance – mine is not an idle talk,- I have struggled to my utmost hitherto to gain a little to my support through my own efforts and the help of friends and neighbours to have a sort of independence but it now fails me – I am distracted with an obstinate cough, an Asthma, and Blind from my birht, and 74 years of Age – the Gentlemen may naturally conclude I shall not trouble them long for I am gradually sinking into the Grave – and the Weather in this part is very severe & Tempestuous, - and every thing is dear, even a Bucket of Water, I cannot obtain without paying for it

Born blind, Brown noted that she had for most of her life managed to maintain a 'sort of independence' through the making of matchboxes, a task which was put-out to domestic workers by match manufacturers for much of the nineteenth-century (King and Timmins 2001). Periodically helped by neighbours, Brown had lived in her own rented house and done her own chores. She did not construct herself and was not constructed by others as disabled. Now, as several illnesses combined in old age she found herself at last unable to avoid asking for parish support. Blindness, then, was on its own not a sufficient reason for Brown to apply for welfare or for the parish to respond. Faced with this conjunction of circumstances the parish paid arrears of rent and small ongoing allowance until Brown's death, which was in her own home some five years later.

During this chapter we have encountered intriguing and at times entertaining letters written by or on behalf of those who were blind or who had failing sight. As historical documents they are an important way into the thinking and detailed experiences of ordinary people who have for so long been submerged in historical analysis of big places, important people and broad processes and structures. But these narratives also surely offer something more? We are, in the late 2010s, becoming a society in which there will be more aged people, many more of them will be alone, and where there is likely to be an avalanche of care needs associated with failing or lost sight. Dilemmas that were common to our historical counterparts will re-emerge. Indeed, we see them being played out in Parliament and the media every day: What should the nature and scope of medical care be, and how much of that care can we expect the State to pay for? How should the welfare state respond to economic and social needs exacerbated by poor sight? What might an appropriate welfare package look like? Should our welfare system move from one funded out from central taxation to one based upon social insurance? And what role should families, friends, and neighbours play in supporting those with poor and deteriorating sight? The nineteenth-century, we have argued, was the last in which deteriorating and lost sight simply had to be lived with and managed (Snow 2006). In the 2020s we will return to such an age. Against this backdrop, the refusal of the State (in the guise of parish officers) and paupers to construct visual impairments into 'disability' is interesting and important. Equally, and having demurred from creating 'disability', the fact that parishes invariably sought to tailor welfare payments to the detailed circumstances of the individual and almost invariably in partnership with other stakeholders, might begin to flag up a different way of thinking about visual impairment for the future. At the core of future State policy for those with visual impairments in Britain will necessarily be a conversation about degrees of ability on the one hand and how to increase the effectiveness of the connection between those with visual impairment, the labour market, and their communities on the other. Such conversations, as we have seen, would have been part of the wallpaper for State officials in the nineteenth-century.

Chapter 3: Deafness

In the last chapter we dealt with historic and current issues around blindness, noting that historical communities refused to construct a loss or lack of sight as 'disability'. Rather, they thought in terms of degrees of *ability* and sought to create a partnership between individual, family and State in order to ameliorate the socio-economic effects of sensory impairment. In this chapter on deafness we continue that broad theme, once again using pauper letters, this time allied with other socio-medical sources, to throw light on the detailed experiences and attitudes of historical actors and the lessons we might draw for modern policy dilemmas. In particular, we focus on three different groups of the 'deaf': those born without hearing; people who lost their hearing during childhood, youth or childbearing adulthood, often through industrial noise, disease or accident; and the aged, increasing inexorably in absolute numbers and as a proportion of the population in later nineteenth-century Britain. For these groups, the potential negative consequences of deafness or poor hearing were as strong as they are today: hearing problems often translated into speech problems and could thus lead to multi-layered exclusion from socio-cultural life; voicelessness might lead to powerlessness in the face of local and national State apparatus which in the nineteenth century was growing rapidly (Higgs 2004); and absent, lost or compromised hearing could easily feed into an inability to train for work, garner skills and hold down a job, leading to weak family economies and ultimate long-term dependence upon the State. In the nineteenth-century this meant reliance on the Old Poor Law parish or the New Poor Law Union with its workhouses (Hollen Lees 1998).

For historical figures the range of questions that these potential experiences throw up share much with modern policy dilemmas: How should the deaf construct themselves and how should they be constructed by others? What should the proper balance be in ameliorating conditions between individual, family or community and State? How does deafness or poor hearing translate into the language of 'disability'? We can expect such questions to gain strength in the modern context over the next few years. The number of children born deaf has diminished over the course of the twentieth-century, something primarily associated with embryo-screening for genetic conditions which might have a knock-on effect for hearing. Similarly, the decline of epidemic disease and the endemic diseases of childhood (in the early twentieth-century) and the rise of health and safety legislation (in the later twentieth-century) have reduced the number of people losing their hearing in childhood and early adulthood. This reversal is almost certainly temporary given the inexorable rise of 'noise' in the modern era and with it the advance of conditions such as tinnitus. At the other end of the age spectrum, the twenty-first century shares with the 1800s, as we saw in the last chapter, a rapidly ageing population and with it an increasingly deaf sub-group of people, often in situations where loss of hearing is one of a suite of physical and mental impairments. How we fashion policies to deal with this group in particular is as problematic as it is current, and in this chapter, we suggest that historical experiences might once more be brought to bear.

We start, then, with that sub-group of people who were deaf from, or very soon after, birth. There is of course no way of knowing how big this group was in nineteenth-century society. The 1861 census recorded 12,236 'deaf mutes' living in England and Wales, almost all of whom would have been deaf from birth. This figure, however, is likely to be the tip of a very large iceberg. Other census categories – the term 'idiot' for instance – were also likely to include people who were deaf or hard of hearing from birth. Moreover, it is likely that many parents in crowded poorer districts, already disproportionately likely not to fill in the nineteenth-century census (Higgs 1989), simply did not record hearing problems amongst their children. Some at least still regarded such impairments as an act of God or as part of the family wallpaper and where we 'discover' such children it is often by accident through sources which do not reflect directly on them or on their deafness. Such is the case of James Smith:

> a Parishioner of yours is in this [work]House in a wretched state of Venereal disease. He is about 30 years old was born deaf in your parish where his parents John and Elizabeth Smith belonged & were both buried by your parish having been previously allowed 2/- about 12 years ago. The Pauper was hired a year ago to John Haughter of College Wood in Your Parish Timber Merchant & never

required a settlement elsewhere. Be kind enough to say whether you will pay for his maintenance & cure in this House having him discharged when able – or if you require us to deal with him under a Susp'd Order.

These are the words of the vestry clerk attached to the Birmingham Poor Law Union workhouse in 1839. The deaf James Smith had turned into a deaf adult, but one who had been able to hold down a job (presumably as a labourer) at a timber merchant until struck down by syphilis. The fact of his venereal disease, a common enough occurrence in Victorian Britain, is what brings his deafness into the ambit of the historian (Bates 2013). This sort of invisibility for those born deaf should not surprise us. As Dr Watson, headmaster of the Old Kent Road Asylum for the Deaf and Dumb (see figure 3.1) reminds us:

> In no instance of original deafness that has come under his notice, has there been any visible imperfection in the external ear. When a child is born deaf, therefore, or totally loses its hearing, there remains nothing for those to whom nature or providence has confided the care of it, but patient acquiescence in the defect; or, which happily has been found practicable to participate the perceptions through other senses, to supply the loss as far as respects the acquisition of speech and language. Persons born deaf are, in fact, neither depressed below, nor raised above, the general scale of human nature, as regards their dispositions and powers, either body or mind. They are human beings, individually differing from their kind, only by accidental defect; this defect is not such as to disturb the course of nature in the first stage of the growth of the mental faculties, though, while it operates as a bar to the acquisition of language, it retards, and almost precludes their expansion after this stage (Curtis 1829).

While Watson made a link between deafness and mental capacity that we might consider tenuous today, his wider point about deaf children and their later incarnation as deaf adults being an indistinguishable part of the socio-cultural landscape, is an important one.

Figure 3.1 Engraving of the Deaf and Dumb Asylum, 1816.

Source: Drawn and Engraved by I.C. Varrall for the Walks through London.
The deaf and dumb Asylum, Kent Road. Wellcome Collection

It has wide resonance with community histories, collective
biographies taken by nineteenth-century amateur historians and
memoirs in which people reflected back on their families and
communities from the vantage point of old age. In these sources, the
deaf have a constant and often significant presence, such that at the
very broadest level we can surmise that few people would not have
known someone with a hearing impairment. The disjuncture between
this observation and the limited numbers of deaf people, particularly
the congenitally deaf, traced in census records, is clear.

The explanations for this situation are multiple. In part, we
witness the impact of growth in the number of institutions specifically
for the accommodation and training of deaf children from the later
eighteenth-century (Hulonce 2014; Mangion 2012; Borsay 2007).
George Bartley in 1871 explored the previous three censuses and
found that the deaf educated in a specialised institution were more

likely to be in employment than a blind person who had been through a similar training scheme. Of the 2,039 people identified only 106 were officially classed as paupers while the rest were in a wide range of diverse occupations, which included engravers, artists, blacksmiths, conveyancers, domestic servants, miners, carpenters and even civil servants (Bartley 1871). It was, in other words, easier for deaf children and deaf adults (with appropriate support) to become invisible to the machinery of Government. There is also, however, something more. The majority of those born deaf or becoming deaf very soon after birth could not have ended up in or passed through specialist institutions. Most of these places were funded through philanthropic donation and subscription and had both limited places and episodic funding crises. It is necessarily the case, then, that deaf children and the young adults that they became lived out their lives in family, community or workhouse contexts. Against this backdrop, and as we saw powerfully for blindness in the last chapter, there is a clear nineteenth century narrative that the deaf were constructed and constructed themselves in terms of degrees of ability rather than inability.

Some sense of this is to be found in attempts by families and communities to apprentice deaf children, allowing them to build the skills required for independent life in the nineteenth-century individual and family economy. It is easy to assume that communities in particular would have taken the quickest and easiest route to divesting themselves of responsibility for the future welfare of deaf children. In fact, and as Katrina Honeyman has also observed (Honeyman 2007), the parish officers who ran the welfare system often took considerable care in placing such children and then monitoring their welfare and development. In our work, for instance, we have often found deaf children sent out on 'trial' before an apprenticeship fee was agreed with the person concerned. This allowed parish officers and third parties to calibrate the investment premium needed over and above standard apprenticeship fees for the training of someone with a hearing impairment. Similarly, it was not the case that either parishes or parents simply 'dumped' deaf children into the first training opportunity that they could find. Rather, there is clear and persistent evidence that certain trades (carpentry, metalworking, straw plaiting, tailoring, shoemaking etc) were seen to be suited to people with hearing impairments and others (domestic services; railway work etc) were not. While work was seen as a solution to potential lifelong dependence in the nineteenth-century (much as it is in modern disability policy) this was carefully calibrated and planned work, and as part of a process in which welfare and the 'right' work were carefully fused together.

We rarely encounter the voices of congenitally deaf children in ego-documents (Tomkins 2013; Humphries 2010) but such voices become more common as they transition to adulthood and family life. Such for instance was William Lloyd, writing from Oxford in 1832. He needed to let his parish of settlement know that:

> In consequence of Extreme distress, I am obliged once more to make application for assistance. My wife is very ill and not able to do for the family and I am Rendered so weak by my Debility that I am not able to support myself and a wife and four children I have always done my best endeavour to support them being deaf but want of trade and ability is my only prevention such a family as mine I find is Very Expensive Its not Vituals alone that suffices there are other Expensive things wanted such as Clothes Bedding &c and all to be depended on from one pair of hands of a Debilitated Constitution... I am at this time in Debt and it is impossible that we can go on in this manner any longer. Had I got Health and strength I would not trouble you for assistance but only for work, but I shall never be able to do any kind of Labourous work no more and I am quite tired of my Miserable Existence.

Lloyd applied for welfare not because he had been deaf from birth but because of his wife's illness, his own ill-health ('debility'), high prices and underemployment ('want of trade'). Indeed, we learn of congenital deafness in a positive sense: that Lloyd had managed to learn a trade and build a family notwithstanding deafness and that if he was relieved now in this dire circumstance he would become independent once more. The want of ability to which he referred spoke to his health condition rather than his sensory impairment. Lloyd is in turn typical of most letter writers who reference a lifelong hearing issue. For this group, being deaf was seemingly no bar to full participation in the economic sphere. Of course, the 'stock' of the deaf in any community was also periodically augmented by a second group of people: those who became deaf during the family building life cycle and prior to what we might recognise as old age. In some cases, hearing loss and reduction was temporary. Thus, Elizabeth Perkins, writing to the overseers of Pangbourne in Berkshire noted in 1828 that:

> This comes in my Duty to you Hoping to find you in good Health I have not been able to get of bed for above this week I have got a violent cold in my Head and now deaf also I can't see so well and I Hope you will consider and send me more money for I cannot do with that I Have the Last you sent I had to pay sixpence for carriage and I have got A doctor to Pay and you have not thought to send any more all the winter and I should like to have my money every month.

In this case, deafness was almost certainly a symptom, the cold having caused a build-up of fluid in the middle ear and making it difficult for sounds to travel efficiently from the outer ear to the eardrum. Modern diagnosis would also suggest that congestion can cause infections which exacerbate the problem, and the fluid can stay trapped in the middle ear for days, weeks or months causing hearing loss. Yet her letter is also revealing; Perkins already had sight impairment and could not have known her additional hearing problems would be temporary. The two conditions in partnership undermined her ability and caused her now to apply to her community for further support. The parish officers in their turn recognised the need for immediate and generous support – replying on the same day - while there was still hope that the passing of an underlying infection might restore a higher degree of ability. This speed and flexibility gives some hint of one of the lessons of the past for modern disability policy.

Hearing impairment amongst the young and middle aged was not always temporary. A range of background circumstances – explosions, infections, occupational noise, assault, alcohol and drugs – could have fundamental consequences for auditory ability. For those that could afford it the Victorian period witnessed an expansion in the use of hearing aids, including ear trumpets (figure 3.2) which worked by amplifying sound, as a partial solution to acquired hearing loss. These are the words of Harriet Martineau:

> The first thing which we are disposed to give up is the very last which we ought to relinquish – society … Social communication must be kept up through all its pains, for the sake of our friends as well as our own … Society is the very last thing to be given up; but it must be sought (and I say it with deep sympathy for those of you to whom the effort is new) under a bondage of self-denial, which annihilates for a time almost all the pleasure. Whatever may be our fate, - whether we may be placed besides a lady who cannot speak above her breath, or a gentleman who shouts till everybody turns to see what is the matter; whether one well-meaning friend says across the room, in our behalf 'do tell that joke over again to…. And all look to see how we laugh when they have done; or another kind person says 'how I wish you could hear that song' or 'those sweet nightingales' if we happen to be out of doors, whether any or all these things and sayings befall us, we must bravely go on taking our place in society.

Martineau was born into an upper middle-class family in Norwich and throughout her life became increasingly deaf. Over time her identity became closely associated with her ear trumpet. When she took an abolitionist stand against slavery it made her too visible and she took to hiding it away to privatise her impairment. Despite being mainly educated at home Martineau was an adept and professional writer, a career which she took up in earnest when family fortunes failed in the 1820s. Although her work was closely tied to the social and political events of the day she has been perceived as a social and political campaigner for many, including deaf minority groups, until her death in 1876. For those who could not afford or did not want to use technology, sign language was also a possibility. Yet at the same time it was also exclusionary, contributing to the 'othering' of deaf people in a nineteenth-century societal context where sign language held an interstitial position between human speech and animal gesture (Esmail 2013).

Figure 3.2 A doctor attempting to alert a farmer to an accident.

Source: Etching, unknown artist. Wellcome Collection.

In the case of most ordinary and poor people confronting hearing loss, it seems that simply 'living with it' was the modus operandi. Poor law sources provide almost no evidence of the State actively seeking to fund treatment to restore hearing. This silence is interesting because, if we take the late twentieth-century epidemic of hearing loss and impairment due to work related noise as a yardstick, it would be reasonable to expect a significant sub-group of the nineteenth-century population to have been affected. Letters from employers to the welfare authorities are more revealing. Often written in response to need amongst their employees due to trade downturn (and thus unemployment or short-time working), these letters sometimes mention sensory impairments as a tangential issue to the main point.

27

The deaf appear here more frequently than perhaps they should, suggesting that employers were not afraid to take on deaf workers or to retain those who became deaf while in their employment. They were, in other words, flexible in relation to impairments well before any legislation compelled them to be. In this sense, work really was for the nineteenth-century deaf individual, a viable alternative identity to 'disability' (Gulliver 2017).

This was, ostensibly at least, less the case for a third group of people in nineteenth-century society: those who became deaf due to a range of accumulating conditions relating to old age. James Richards, writing to the overseers of the parish of Thrapston. He noted that:

> Necessity compels me to trouble you with a few lines which I hope you will excuse to inform you how distressed me and my wife labours under, my earnings being so small when I am able to work together with the one shilling a week you are pleased to allow me is not nearly sufficient for a maintenance to us both renders it absolutely necessary to state to you that unless the gentlemen of your parish as well as mine can allow me something more these hard times that what you do at present, we must be under the necessity of coming to your poorhouse as out of it we cannot do any longer without further support as rent and fireing takes us full 3 shillings a week and what my wife earns when trade is good is very small, and none at this time as well as for a long time back there has been little or nothing doing in the ribbon business, therefore I do earnestly implore further aid and assistance from you when in such hard times as these you no doubt are quite aware of my privations in hearing and lameness and if spared till some time in February I am of the age of 75 and that of my poor wife upwards of 70 so gentlemen under all these consideration you will be pleased to comply with our earnest wishes either in the one way or the other and that without loss of time and I remain anxiously waiting for the result from you.

Richards had clearly lost his hearing over time ('privations') and been subsisting for a while on a mixture of his earnings from work, those of his wife and a small parish allowance. Now as other physical problems overtook him ('lameness') and his wife sank into illness he called upon his place of belonging ('your parish as well as mine') to help him further in what would then have been regarded perfectly properly as extreme old age.

The poor law sources are replete with examples like James Richards and there can be no doubt at all that the rapid ageing of the population in the later nineteenth-century occasioned by fertility decline on the one hand and lower disease-related mortality on the other created a substantial and growing group of aged people in most communities (Garrett, Reid, Schürer and Szreter 2001). For these people, deterioration in sensory abilities would have been significant and relatively rapid. Against this backdrop, the core lessons to be drawn from the case of James Richards are important. First, he at no point in this or other letters constructed himself as disabled or placed his sensory and other impairments at the centre of his appeal for support. Rather Richards focussed on factors which compromised his abilities to work and care for his wife. In turn, and second, when confronted by this claim the welfare authorities in Thrapston responded quickly by increasing his allowance in the hope that they could extend his working life. At no point between this letter of 1833 and the death of both old people in 1836 did officials understand Richards to be completely unable or disabled. Sensory impairment was merely a background condition and by no means the most important.

Our historical sources are important in their own right. They challenge the broad-brush conclusions of new disability histories which focus on the supposed othering and exclusion of those with sensory impairments in the period before legal rights to fairer or equal treatment were fashioned (Borsay 2005). For the deaf at least we see the exact opposite, with welfare authorities going out of their way (and often at no little expense) to ensure the proper integration of those deaf from birth into the society and labour market. As deaf children grew into deaf adults and their numbers were augmented by those losing their hearing absolutely or by degrees, so the same welfare authorities resolutely resisted any linguistic, categorical or actual rendering of people with hearing impairments as disabled. Nor did those experiencing such impairment construct themselves in this way. Sensory problems were so much part of the socio-economic and familial wallpaper that they usually appear in our sources as matters of fact or tangential reporting and nothing more. This is not to argue that the deaf or hard of hearing were always treated well. There are plenty of examples, notably where hearing loss fed into speech impediment as opposed to muteness, where they were not. But the deaf were not powerless and they had agency as well as advocacy from the very many who wrote to welfare authorities on their behalf. They had, in other words, a moral right to have their cases weighted and judged, irrespective of the exact letter of the law. This right was valuable, akin to a currency, and could be protected by focussing in engagement with welfare authorities on degrees of ability rather than degrees of inability.

These observations matter for current disability policy. Successive governments of all political hues have regarded participation in the labour market as a way to confront the inter-connected problems of the othering of those with sensory impairments on the one hand and their relative poverty on the other. Policies of 'reasonable adjustment', requirements to interview those with protected characteristics and funding for employers taking on people with sensory or physical impairments have gone some way to realising government ambition. Yet these gains have sometimes proved superficial and reversible as job markets tighten, funding for disability-work initiatives dries up and training opportunities for those with sensory impairments fail to become self-generating. Our sources point to the need for a more flexible and rapid 'conveyor belt' approach to the link between work, welfare and impairment, one in which small interventions can keep people in work or deal with contextual factors which might otherwise thrust impairment into disability. This flexibility will become ever more important as the proportion of the population with hearing impairments rises rapidly in the early twenty-first century much as it did in the later nineteenth. The inevitable rise in the state pension age and rising pensioner poverty will progressively increase the number of people with hearing problems in the labour market and require a different architecture for the relationship between work and welfare. More widely, lost or rapidly declining hearing associated with age will have to be confronted with a new narrative of degrees of ability rather than disability, and with a new model of moral instead of just legal rights. In this sense we have much to learn from the past.

Chapter 4: Physical Impairment

Over the last two chapters we have dealt with aspects of sensory impairment. In practice, these were often in the past (and are still now) yoked together with a range of other physical and mental conditions as part of a broader experience which shaped life at the individual level (Hampton 2016). Equally, however, the residents of most nineteenth-century communities and neighbourhoods would have been well aware of significant numbers of people with discrete physical impairments - lost or compromised limbs (from birth and by accident), what contemporaries called 'decline' or weaknesses associated with disease and old age, chronic problems created by childbirth, and the neurological conditions that were often associated with working conditions in nineteenth-century trades – which were on display constantly as part of everyday life and interaction.

Clearly this is a huge area of enquiry and we can only scratch the surface here. But scratching the surface reveals something very important. That is, the conditions that created physical impairments were both common and multiplying in the nineteenth-century: wars led to lost or useless limbs; male midwives with a penchant for using crude forceps compromised young bones (Wilson 2007); tuberculosis led to amputations; working in mines and factories led to people being, as was the common term in the nineteenth century, 'dreadfully mangled'; transport and other accidents maimed more often than they killed; children got into dreadful scrapes when they played; and strokes, cancers and other 'modern' diseases coming to the fore as part of the nineteenth-century mortality transition could easily result in physical impairments on the road to death or recovery. Some occupations were particularly hazardous, as these words from John Brooker, sent from London to his home parish of Pangbourne (Berkshire) in an undated letter sometime in the early 1800s, indicate:

My Business *you well know* is very pernicious to most Men that follow it after they have been a few years in the employ. But there is no doing without Painters, for Paint not only preserves but ornaments a Building without which the best of Structures would soon look mean, and filthy, as well come to decay. But it is a Misfortune to them who are brought up to such a Trade that in the prime of life, lose the Use of Limbs by a relaxation of their Nerves, attended with Violent Coughs, Asthmas, &c. And have only to *linger out a few miserable Months, or years,* in Anguish, and Pain of Body, which Renders the miserable Objects, unable to get that Relief whereby they might be able to get their bread. Finding myself better I came to London last May twelve months, in hopes I might be able to follow my business again, having no other way of getting my living. But I had not long tried to work, when my Complaints returned worse than ever, and I have been above twelvemonths, and only done Seven days work put it altogether. As often as I have tried to work for two, or three hours, I have been so ill as to be oblidged to leaved my work, and take to my Bed, where I am confined most of my time, and am now so Bad, I do not expect ever to be any better in this Life, as no Physition can administer to me the least Relief.

While Brooker still had his limbs, working with leaded paint (now of course banned across the world) had given him uncontrollable shaking because of neurological damage (Mills and Adderley 2017). He had helped himself as much as he could, but this had now become a chronic condition which prevented him from working for any length of time. The sense of hopelessness in this letter (no doctor could administer relief because this condition was inexorably associated with the work itself) is palpable and Brooker signified a transition from a degree of ability to one of inability or even disability by noting that he was now confined to bed. This signal to the parish authorities is familiar from other chapters, with the withdrawal from public life and gaze the ultimate yardstick of dependence. Presumably Brooker was cared for by the wife that we know he had because she was mentioned in other (later letters) about the case. Presumably too his story would have been a matter of discussion and knowing nods in the locality. At the very least the arrival of people delivering parish cash would have been a signal that all was not well in the Brooker household. In turn, stories like this could be reproduced from our sources in striking numbers. The key point for *Disability Matters* is that those with physical impairments were to be found all around families and communities in the period we are talking about. Quite simply it was 'normal' to see and know such people in a way that is perhaps unfamiliar today.

This state of affairs did not always play into sympathy, consideration and support. Some contemporaries at least were suspicious of those with physical impairments who ended up begging, as wandering vagrants or in some urban 'jobs' (such as crossing sweeping or hawking from a basket) that sat uneasily between gainful employment and aggressive begging (Ferguson 2015; the modern equivalent would be people washing windows at traffic lights). After all, even lost limbs could be faked by the street beggar and more widely there were enduring suspicions that those on the streets and exhibiting physical impairment could and should be in work. Much as with modern begging there were in the nineteenth-century episodic 'moral panics' (Lemmings and Walker 2009) which resulted in a harshening of attitudes towards welfare recipients and beggars, something which disproportionately affected those with physical impairments. At such times, having a missing leg, crushed arm or useless limb, and even more exhibiting the effects of neurological damage, could be elided uncomfortably with criminality as problematic people were swept off the streets. Yet, such moral panics were, as with their modern counterparts, generally short-lived because to treat those with physical impairments in this way flew in the face of their significant and increasing numbers in visible public life.

Links to the modern context are compelling. Over the last two decades we have seen an explosion in the scale and intensity of physical impairment, at least measured by the level of spending on broadly defined disability, caring, enabling and accessibility benefits. Much of this is correlated with the mobility and impairment problems associated with old age and we might expect these to multiply rapidly as our current population ages. Other factors have also begun to contribute, however, with the rapid spread of diabetes, obesity and arthritis all carrying current and (even more) future consequences for physical impairment. It is no accident, then, that governments have sought to tighten the eligibility for benefits associated with physical impairments, switching from a disability to an ability test of the sort which would have been familiar to our nineteenth-century writers and which we have traced consistently in prior chapters. However, we view such attempts, it is clear that an epidemic of physical impairment will raise important questions about the remit of the State versus the individual, the construction of disability by different stakeholders, and the proper role of families and communities in caring for individuals. These questions are universal, and they applied as keenly in the nineteenth-century as they do today and will tomorrow.

Looking at historical experiences, then, provides one way to think more expansively about how society could and should interact with those who have varying degrees of physical impairment. We can develop this idea by looking at the words of Charles Simcock, written in a letter from Ashton-under-Lyne (Cheshire) to Hulme in Manchester:

> Gentlemen. I think it my duty to inform you that I have totally lost the use of my right leg and have to use a crutch to support me the few hours I'm able to go about during the day and consequently have not been able this last six months to hearn food sufficient for myself and family. From the repeated enquiries made after me and the impudence of the female Sarah Tomlinson to my wife whilst I was absent at the Doctors I'm inclined to think a false statement and rong impression may be given of my infirmity I therefore beg to refer you to Dr Wood whome I've been under three months without his being able to cure me or to Dr Winsor of Manch'r that I'm at present under for a corroboration of what I have stated – should you require any further satisfaction of the truth of my severe affliction I will wait upon you at the office any time you may be pleased to appoint. With many thanks for favours you have shown me during so long a sickness, I am your humble Servant.

The letter is undated, but subsequent correspondence tells us it must have been written sometime in the early summer of 1837. In later letters we learn that Simcock's complaint was 'chronic Rheumatism'. For him a physical impairment threatened to become chronic notwithstanding his attempts to get a cure from local doctors. His ability to work was compromised and therefore his status as a head of household. Not to be able to put food on the table led to questionable manhood (Delap, Griffin and Wills 2009). Yet Simcock also realised that his condition, because it was not a visible physical impairment even if it had visible consequences, might lead to him being labelled a malingerer when enquiries were made about him. In this letter he sought to set the record straight, asking local welfare officials for a bit of help in tiding him over. In a later letter he noted that 'Mr Wood Surgeon of this town … promises fair to cure me if I can take a little rest' and this being so he would be able to (literally, as he was a printer) 'stand' his work. Simcock clearly did not construct himself as disabled and nor did his parish, which ended up paying him an allowance to try and get him back on his feet (as it were) over a six-month period. With his own precarious work, the help of friends and neighbours and a small job for his wife, he was able to maintain his independence. On the other hand, his first letter clearly flags up to us a fear that his right to welfare would be contested, something that might be familiar to those applying for or renewing what we now call Disability Living Allowance.

Yet Simcock's fear and experience of surveillance were not 'normal'. This letter from Joseph Richards, living in Coventry but writing back to his home parish of Thrapston (Northamptonshire) on 28 December 1825, is far more representative:

> Sir,
> I am truly sorry to be so troublesome to you and the gentlemen of my parish for my complaint that I have on me is so bad in my right arm that I cannot do any sort of work at all and likewise the complaint which I went into the infirmary at Leicester is almost as bad as ever that it comes down as bad as ever and I cannot keep it up so that it is with great difficulty I can get about and am sorry to say that at this time my wife is so ill that I don't expect her to live one hour from another which causes me to be in a distressed situation and through the weaving trade being so bad that my two daughters which is the mean [main] stay of our support wholly causes me to make this application as we have nothing to depend upon only the small allowance which you are so good as to allow me and hope you will be so graciously pleased to make my sad case known to the Gentlemen and that they will be so

kind as to allow me 1/6 more per week until the Trade gets better and then we will with the allowance you already give us do as well as we can

It is unclear what the problem with Richards's arm was, but less than a year later he was to have it amputated. Here he catalogued a series of events and experiences in addition to his physical impairment which, together, justified an extension of his existing welfare allowance. The fact that he already had an allowance is important, suggesting that the officers of Thrapston deemed his physical impairment sufficiently worrying to enter into a partnership with the family in order to allow him to live in independence. Indeed, a striking thing about almost all of our many letters dealing with physical impairment is that both the poor person and their parish usually worked together, and with shared resources, to allow continued domestic residence and thus avoid institutions like the workhouse. There are many reasons to think this sense and practice of partnership is also what the future will hold as Britain faces an explosion of physical impairments at the same time as we enter a prolonged period of low economic and taxation growth.

The sense that nineteenth-century officials and the society they represented saw physical impairment as conferring deservingness of at least a share of communal resources can be seen in the letter of Thomas Haywood, overseer of Lichfield, who was writing to his counterpart in Lilleshall on 10 March 1817:

> Sir, above you have the Am^t of money advanced to your pauper, which hope you will send by the bearer hereof, Mr John Fernyhough, whose receipt shall be your discharge, poor old Dorling has a very bad hand, which I fear must be Amputated we have sent him to the Infirmary so you will have no Doctor to pay, the Daughter is still getting worse with fits, the old woman is almost worn out with fatigue, and you may depend on it they are Miserable objects and should have something to buy the daughter some Cloathing

Haywood was in this case doing more than simply reporting the physical impairment of Richard Dorling. Rather, we can trace feeling for his predicament with these accumulated misfortunes and an active sense of advocacy on his behalf with the settlement parish in Staffordshire (King and Jones 2016). The suspicion with which Charles Simcock feared he would be viewed is missing here. Haywood wrote again on 20 April 1817 to say that: 'I must beg leave to tell you that the old man has had his hand Amputated therefore he is unable to do any kind of business, and the consequence will be, you will have the family to keep entirely'. This was some way from the truth, since Dorling himself, his family, neighbours and the parish came together to form a patchwork of support and self-support which allowed the family to retain independence, in the process keeping a daughter beset with epileptic fits away from full economic dependence on her parish. While modern, rule-based, welfare systems of the sort practiced in the UK penalise the ability of family and friends to support those with impairments, this discretionary but morally based poor law, rewarded and encouraged it.

In turn, and as with the sensory impairments that we have analysed in earlier chapters, our source material is replete with a sense that parishes and the poor thought about physical impairment against the backdrop of an implicit and well-understood scale of ability and inability. We see this clearly in the case of Sarah Giles, who was writing from her home in Norwich to her settlement parish of Rothersthorpe (Northamptonshire) on 18 February 1804:

> Gentlmn I humbly ask that you look to my case and stand as my last frend in this wurld You Know of me I am Sarah Jiles and my farther was Samuel Jiles the shoeman and I left you some time since but you know me Sir and I have not been able to walk as you know since my accident Sir and have to be pushed around when I can but I am not nor dcrsabled as you might call it but I derpend on selling my little thyngs on the street and this gets me most of my part and with the kind help of my naybours and the indugunce of my landlord and no littel help from my Brother you Knows him Well I can make do but now I have been ill these last wintur munths and I have not bin abul to git about in the snow and can not use the crutches or the wheel in these times and so I am beehind with all ands so will you please kindly show as a frend for just a month as

> I am less able that I may settle some littel deps and keep
> my head up here that I may once again do what I can
> without youre asisternce I am Your Humble servant

Giles had been paralysed in a fall down a disused quarry pit as a girl and we have records of the race to save her life at that time. As an adult of 34 years of age, she now applied for help from her parish, but she assumed that there was a shared understanding that her paralysis did not equate to disability. When the weather was good, and she was healthy, Giles could wheel (presumably in some form of cart of the sort seen in figure 4.1) or crutch herself around selling items from a basket on the street.

This did not make her independent but as a familiar part of a patchwork of making do, this work was important (King 2004). External conditions made her (she presumed the officials who received the letter would acknowledge) less able and when less able she assumed (rightly as it turns out) that the parish would step in temporarily to take up the slack in her income. Like so many modern people with physical impairments, Giles constructed herself as partially able/episodically unable or less able, and wanted, or at least rhetoricised a desire, to be independent of the State. Full, long-term, dependence on welfare was not something that she could envisage.

It would be naïve of us to suggest that the lessons of historical material map seamlessly onto modern conditions and experiences. But nor, as previous chapters have suggested, should we dismiss them. Much like the early nineteenth-century, the early twenty-first will be an age of increasing physical impairment, albeit with slightly different causation. Another common thread is the attitude to welfare sustainability: Both periods witness extensive public discussions of the limits of welfare in relation to its current and future costs and as a philosophical engagement about the limits and extent of rights and obligations (Jones and King 2015). Squaring this circle was and is a challenge. Against this backdrop, three features of our source material are worth further thought as we grapple for modern solutions to the welfare consequences of physical impairment.

Figure 4.1 An old man in a wooden cart writing about the parish of St. Paul Covent Garden, London.

Source: Etching by John Thomas Smith, c.1821. Wellcome Collection.

The first is that people with physical impairments, and the local welfare officials to whom they wrote, did not ever construct themselves as disabled and dependent unless the extent of that impairment confined them to bed or caused them otherwise to withdraw from the public world. Rather, they thought about themselves and were measured on a spectrum of ability and attainment, their position on which might change over time, life-cycle or according to external factors such as unemployment of a family member. Modern official attitudes to physical impairments, as for instance crystallised in new tests for disability-related allowances, do not look very different in a philosophical and practical sense. Intriguingly, though, it is clear that localism in welfare in the early nineteenth-century introduced an element of short-term flexibility and long-term engagement with individual cases which is not apparent now.

A second feature of our material is that welfare was rarely seen, either by our writers or the people receiving their letters, as *the* answer. Almost universally, responses to the impact of physical impairment involved, and were meant to involve, a partnership of friends, neighbours, local State, institutions and the self-help of the individual concerned. In this context, the scale, duration and intensity of benefits was endlessly flexible and specifically calibrated to the changing dimensions of this partnership. Our modern benefit system has lost such flexibility and adaptability at the same time as it has lost its essential localism. Future responses to a rising tide of physical impairment will certainly require a return to this historic mode of thinking.

Finally, our source material suggests that physical impairment was so common and so visible in the nineteenth-century that few people could have been unaffected by it directly or indirectly. This visibility gave the physically impaired poor a moral, rather than just a vague and fragile legal claim on the welfare resources of their communities. As legislation has accumulated and physical impairment has become less visible, so that moral right has deteriorated, and with it support for the benefits paid to this group. With the extent and intensity of physical impairment mounting once again, the importance of moral right may re-emerge as a key feature in public understanding of the role and duty of our State welfare system.

Chapter 5: Mental Impairment

In the last chapter we considered the experience of physical impairment in the nineteenth-century, suggesting that the way that people in this position were constructed, understood, treated and perceived may provide clues for the future development of welfare policy. This chapter turns to the question of mental impairment, which we understand here as an over-arching term encompassing depression, anxiety, so-called personality disorders, degeneration of mental capacity due to encroaching age, and congenital or acquired learning difficulties. While the medical profession only began to effectively and comprehensively label these mental impairments from the later nineteenth-century, prior contemporary terms and phrases – idiot, hysterical, drawn low, feeble-minded, not quite right in the head – give a sense that contemporaries understood at the very broadest level distinctions between different forms of mental health issues.

Against this backdrop, the parallels between the nineteenth and twenty-first centuries in terms of the 'problem' of mental health, are striking. Nineteenth-century British society witnessed enormous structural changes with unprecedented population growth, substantial development in industry (King and Timmins 2001) and a resultant rise in urban conurbations which led to the rapid rise of social isolation, the creation of drug and gang cultures (Davies 1998), dislocation of families and communities and sustained migration and immigration. Even to the most casual of observers, the same basic suite of social problems will be evident in our modern urban society. Some nineteenth-century observers felt that mental health problems had become 'fashionable', particularly amongst women, much as we now worry about the 'copycat' behaviour of young people claiming mental health issues (Logan 1997). Fashionable or not, the nineteenth-century witnessed an explosion of recorded mental impairment amongst all ranks and orders of the population. To some degree this reflected the building of State funded (as opposed to private; Philo 2004) asylums to which 'the mad' could be sent, so that there was a purpose to identifying them in communities and families in the first place (Smith 2007). Whether the incarceration of those with mental ill-health issues across a range from learning difficulties through to violent personality disorders reflects a desire for social control or a genuine belief in the power of increasingly 'moral' treatment of those who ended up in asylums, is a matter of historical debate (Andrews and Digby 2004). What is clear, however, is that more mental health issues were progressively identified and labelled, more of those experiences at the individual level were medicalised and problematized, and that the proportion of the background population experiencing mental health problems escalated. No modern observer could fail to be struck by the clanging resonance between these and modern experiences which tend strongly in the same direction.

Nor do the similarities end here. While it is true that growing numbers of the nineteenth-century 'mad' were incarcerated in lunatic asylums where their conditions were increasingly seen as remediable, many more people with mental health impairments ended up in jail, much as they do today (Storey 2010). And numbers in both institutions were (and are today) dwarfed by those who remain 'cared for' or contained in communities and families. In the nineteenth-century, changing norms of behaviour, increasing urbanisation and thus concentration of people, and a slow reduction in the caring capacities of families linked to the rise of women's work and child education, necessitated the building of asylums. Modern readers will be struck by the resonances with the present day mental ill-health 'system', where the mismatch between finite resources and an exploding 'problem' will inevitably require a radical rethink of how and where we deal with mental health issues.

In this context, our nineteenth-century sources are potentially very illuminating. Thus, even before the systematic rise of State funded County Lunatic Asylums between the 1820s and 1870s, parishes and families found that some institutional provision for the confinement, containment and treatment of 'the mad' was a vital supplement to or substitute for communal and family support. In the example below, the parish officers of Oundle (Northamptonshire) wrote in 1838 to an un-named private asylum to say that:

> We have a person now in our workhouse a confirmed Lunatic and the Poor Law Commissioner desires us to remove her. Under these circumstances our Select vestry have desired me to apply for fourteen shillings per week for her maintenance & clothing as a Pauper. At times she is

quite sane for many days at other times requiring confinement. Your early answer will oblige.

An agreement pertaining to this unnamed woman must have been swiftly reached as we can see from the following letter to Dr Armstrong at the Peckham Lunatic Asylum:

We intend sending by the Oundle coach tomorrow (Monday) the Pauper Lunatic. She will be accompanied by our workhouse master to take care of her and Mr Bonfield one of the Overseers will be in Town and will deliver her into your House sometime the same evening. I think the coach arrives at the 3 Caps Aldgate by about 6 o'clock and I recommend them to take a Coach & go direct with her to your Establishment. You may therefore expect her on Monday evening. The Paper you sent has been regularly signed by the Clergyman, overseer & surgeon as directed by you & Mr Bonfield has it to deliver with the Lunatic.

We do not, of course, know what was 'wrong' with this woman, but the fact that she was already in the Union workhouse under the early New Poor Law suggests either that she was without family or that existing familial and communal arrangements had broken down. Local officials did not seek institutional confinement lightly, not least because it was extraordinarily costly when set against alternatives, something that also in part drove the closure of large mental hospitals in the 1980s. Rather some of our sources suggest a genuine regret at having to seek an institutional solution, and ongoing care about those with mental impairments:

I am desired by our Select Vestry to write to you for some information relative to the admission of a Pauper Lunatic belonging to and residing now in this parish. He is about 22 years of age and has been a millers man by trade and has now been in a decayed state for 3 or 4 months constantly crying and talking but frequently violent he has had the Parish medical man's assistance without any decided improvement and therefore the vestry wish now to place him in some Public Asylum for a short time that

he may have a chance of any benefit that can be procured
to him from a proper treatment. Under these
circumstances I shall feel much obliged by your stating if
he is eligible to yr Establishment & upon what terms and
forms you require and when he would be admitted. Two
medical gentlemen have seen him & both Pronounce him
a fit object for a charity Lunatic Asylum. Awaiting every
particular which you will oblige

These are the words of Henry Roper of the parish of Oundle who was
seeking to incarcerate George Fields as an inpatient at the Bethlem
Hospital in London (Andrews, Briggs, Porter, Tucker and
Waddington 1997). Roper clearly intended that residence in the
asylum would be temporary ('short time'), and indeed Fields was
eventually to return to his home town at least partially cured. We have
been long used to thinking of the nineteenth-century asylum as a place
of permanent confinement (as many eventually did become in the
twentieth-century) but in fact long-term residence in one asylum
context was relatively rare and circulation of patients between
'solutions' (family, workhouses, lodgings, asylums) was normal. In a
modern sense, the lack of this crucial part of the jigsaw for supporting
mental health, the lack in other words of a flexible institutional space
configured in a respite capacity, is usually cited as one of the key
failings when those with mental health issues harm themselves or
others.

A second observation of our data is also important in this
respect. That is, for rapidly changing nineteenth-century society there
were limits to communal and familial support of those with mental
impairments. Some sense of this is to be found in the following letter
sent by Mr Roper of Oundle to the Overseers of Gedney
(Lincolnshire) in March 1835. Roper had received a communication
about the pauper Mr Burney and was:

Requested to see him. Upon the servants making some
remark he knocked them down & ran up stairs cornered
Mrs B into the Dining Room and was only prevented from
other like acts by Mr C's interference. Also going into
Tradesmens shops insisting upon paper & ink to write to
the King, Duke of Wellington and many other noblemen

and our postmaster informs me he went there and requested the same thing as he had much to inform [them] about. Also driving his wife out of the house threatening to murder her & her children and going to W. Burney's to beg information against many people of Robbing without any cause Threatening Distinction of many Persons within the Town. Indeed his Acts were so much like a dangerous Lunatic

Rapid deterioration in Mr Burney's condition was immediately brought to the attention of welfare officers. This and the increasingly public nature of his 'lunacy', such that he was a danger to himself and others, caused families to despair and officials to intervene. In this case Burney ended up in an asylum.

Anthony Harris is another representative example. These are the words of John Mitchell, written in February 1812:

Gentlemen, There is a Family belonging to your Parish, resident here, in a Situation of great Distress – It is that of Anthony Harris, his wife, & 3 children – He has supported himself & Family by his Industry, so long as he had the Power to work; but he became deranged in his Intellect some months ago, & it is now no longer safe to himself & others that he should be permitted to roam at large…A few weeks ago he left his Home, & after wandering about several Days was brought home by the Beadle of Kensington Parish, where he had wandered – On Thursday morning he left his Home again, & has not since been heard of – His poor Wife is half distracted, & after walking yesterday 30 Miles, & making every Inquiry where there was a chance of any Intelligence, is very ill from Anxiety, Fatigue & Distress…If he should return to this place, it will be necessary to place him somewhere in confinement – Indeed it ought to have been done long ago – I will undertake through the Medium of some Friends to procure his admission into St Luke's Hospital, provided you are disposed to indemnify me for the Expence – There must be a Deposit of Six Pounds in the Hands of the Treasurer on his Admission, & 2 Housekeepers must enter into a Bond of 100£ to remove him from the Hospital at the Expiration of the 12 Months, provided he should be deemed incurable –

Harris was indeed sent to an asylum, primarily because his care had moved beyond the capacity of his wife (who was 'very ill from Anxiety, Fatigue & Distress') as well as the community. In December of the same year the hospital reported that 'that there is no Improvement whatever. His bodily Health is good but his Mind remains in the same Sullen State, as when he was first admitted'. Harris was to remain in asylum care for the rest of his life.

Sometimes, it was the sheer cost of dealing with mental impairments that led to families seeking a wider solution. Looking after, watching, confining and buying treatment for 'the mad' could rapidly drain familial coffers both in terms of ready cash and income foregone through an inability to work while providing care (Smith 2012). Even where individuals ended up in institutions (asylums, workhouses etc) families might end up providing supplementary resources which could be draining. These, for instance, are the words of the Derbyshire doctor Edward Wrench, drawn from his diary of 1866:

> With old Mr Sterndale to see his sister Agnes Cooker who is in Dr Dicksons Asylum at Buxton. Sterndale was anxious to see whether his sister could be removed to a cheaper Asylum. I found her just the same as she was when I sent her there four years ago and suggested she should be put into a cheaper class in the same house. I liked the look of the Asylum and of Dr Dickson who is rough mannered but kind.

The fact that the asylum had different classes of accommodation and care (and thus different costs) is interesting and replicated across the private asylum system of the nineteenth-century. The important point for *Disability Matters*, however, is that Mr Sterndale, Agnes Cooker's brother, was paying the bills and finding it a strain.

For a variety of reasons, then, there were limits to familial support and broadly conceived 'care by the community'. The remarkable thing about our nineteenth-century evidence is the speed with which the breakdown of existing arrangements were flagged to the welfare authorities and the rapidity with which they in turn acted either to support and repair them or to find substitute care. While nineteenth-century communities were often beset with wandering vagrants (Croley 1995), the *infrequency* with which obviously 'mad' people were to be found alone on street corners and roads suggests that this support system worked at the broadest level. Jumping forward to the present day, exactly the opposite situation appears to be true. Those with mental impairments and their families and communities frequently complain about the lack of action in cases of deterioration or in light of changed familial circumstances, uncertainty over where to report problems and receive support, and the sheer inflexibility and slothfulness of the mental health 'system'. The signature of broadly conceived disability policy in the twenty-first century is the fact that the system does not listen, something that would have been incomprehensible to our nineteenth-century welfare officers.

In turn, a third observation arising from our data is that there was a recognition albeit often crude, that mental impairments were complex and that the balancing response in the mixed economy of care also needed to be complex. Edward Wrench, our Derbyshire doctor encountered earlier in the chapter, recorded in his diary entry for February 1878 his visit:

> With the Rev J Howard Twist to Northampton to see his wife who is at the asylum. I attended her at Bakewell 3 years ago when she began with puerperal mania she has been at Winslow's [asylum] until lately and she has now dementia. I saw her she did not recognise me. She is thin but well. She was noisy and excited. I also saw Miss Broomhead she was fat and well in bodily health but will not talk & is quite demented occasionally violent.

Wrench's reference to dementia here almost certainly did not reflect the modern usage of the term given that Mrs Howard was clearly of childbearing age. Rather, he is likely to be reporting severe depression or manic depression. Whatever the actual diagnosis, it was clearly the violent tendencies that had led the prolonged residence in a private asylum in this case and that of Miss Broomhead. The fact that Wrench knew two women from his doctoring circuit in the same asylum also, of course, testifies to the epidemic of mental impairment in Victorian England. He himself had personal experience of what was then known as violent lunacy; Wrench had escorted his Uncle Buchan to the Coppice Lunatic Asylum in Nottingham when his aunt was no longer able to control him at home and there was a danger of leaving him in his then residence. Whether as a result of his mental impairment or in a moment of lucidity, within two weeks of his admission Uncle Buchan committed suicide. It was at this point the severity of his 'madness' was truly apparent, but in different circumstances there might have been an even more tragic ending. It transpired that Buchan had once tried to kill his wife 'by mixing broken glass in a draught he asked her to drink saying you must not mind if it hurts you a little'.

Yet the decision of when to turn to institutional confinement (and when to return someone from institutional confinement to a communal or family environment) was almost always finely grained. Indeed, people with mental impairments often remained in their nineteenth-century communities and with active community support and engagement for much longer than we could expect given the option of locking them up in an asylum or sending them to jail. Mr Burney, encountered earlier as a dangerous lunatic, did not automatically experience incarceration, as this letter indicates:

> … the overseers and medical man considered it necessary to have two men always with him and to be fastened to the Bed. But now from Bleeding & medicine he is so much better that he is allowed to go about with one man to look after him and I think now he is only mad upon some points but he is certainly not in a fit state to be at large. The letters he wrote were not badly done but his acts after days back all indicating an unsoundness of mind. Now he goes out he will get into the Public Houses is possible and of course all stimulus should be avoided that if he was away from those haunts the Better.

Even a casual reflection on these words is enlightening. The local welfare system had paid for a period of intensive treatment by a doctor and at the same time two (likely expensive) men to watch over him so as to prevent personal harm or danger to others (King 2014).

Recognising the possibility of recovery as indicated by actions (itself a significant observation), the official then paid another man full time to 'go about' with Burney so as to keep him away from alcohol which by inference was deemed to be a cause in his mental instability, much as it has a role in mental health today. Such intensive, expensive and long-term action, calibrated carefully to the depth of Burney's madness or at least symptoms, reveals a complex understanding of the mental impairment as well as a determination to 'do the best' in terms of spending cash and time for the pauper concerned. By the end of his life Burney had moved seamlessly between asylum, workhouse, familial care, boarding, independence and back again, a personal journey traced, recorded and orchestrated by the welfare system with which he or his family were episodically in contact.

This sort of complex understanding, and calibration was also played out in cases where the form of mental impairment was more amorphous. Edward Wrench recorded the case of one John Cocker:

> At work as usual all day & called out at 9pm to young John Cocker found him in a hysteric epileptic fit with flushed face suffused eyes and rapid pulse tried to bleed him but could find no vein. Douched him with some benefit. He came home at 8.30 & said two men had been putting him in the water (he was wet) and laughing very much fell down in this fit he had had some drink … Tuesday – he can remember nothing of what passed for several hours before the fit came on last night. He is quite sensible but weak & sore this morning

To the modern reader it will be obvious that John Cocker was suffering from a form of epilepsy, but Wrench had little understanding of the physiological and neurological construction of the condition. He did not seek to refer Cocker to a hospital or other institution, even though he could easily have done so (Lekka 2015). Rather, Wrench undertook palliative intervention and consigned him back to the care of the family, emphasising forcibly the operation of a mixed economy of care.

We do not know what became of Cocker, but for other people exhibiting signs of epilepsy there are more complete stories. Some certainly ended up in nineteenth-century asylums and under the surgeon's knife. Others resided long-term in workhouses as families disintegrated around epileptics previously cared for in a domestic environment. These were, however, exceptional cases. In most instances welfare officials under both the Old and New Poor Law sought to intervene in order to generate continuity of care and the continued presence of epileptics in communities and work situations. As the overseer of Rothersthorpe (Northamptonshire) wrote to his counterpart in Cambridge when they corresponded about the epilepsy of Hannah Brown:

> You write that her fitts have been growing in number and length and I am sorry for it. I authorise you to send her as one of your own paupers to whatever hospital or man [doctor] may best suit and to let us know of the expense which we will reimburse. This is a sad case but to be expected as she has had Fitts since she was a small girl. Our parish would not want to see her come at last to some workhouse or asylum and if you think fit you may send her home at our expense and we shall lodge her with one of the nurses in the parish that she might have the most proper and humane attention for as long as this is possible.

The concepts that wind through this short but important letter – humanity, sadness, the desire to act to maintain Brown in her community, shying away from institutional care, and a recognition that Brown's mental impairment was part of a long story – are important. Indeed, turned on their head, such approaches tell us all of the things that modern mental health and welfare services are perceived *not* to do. Moreover, all of this trouble was taken over a woman who had no family (the officials offered to board her with a nurse, not with her family as he would have done if they were still alive) and for whom it would have been all too easy and possibly cheaper to seek an immediate institutional solution. The long history of Brown with her parish mattered very much in this case, and it is arguably the failure of modern welfare services to have and understand a history with mental patients and their families which has brought them into such disrepute.

The two guiding principles of the reforms to support individuals with mental impairments in the late 1980s and 1990s were: that personal independence, rather than residence in mental hospitals and ex-asylums, was possible; and that it could be secured through a matrix of services and entitlements at the community level. It became apparent very soon thereafter that this matrix was failing and that the ideal of community support had in fact disintegrated into community abandonment. Subsequent politicians of all parties have failed to grasp two essential problems with the system in addition to the failure over 40 years to 'join the dots'. The first is that treating mental impairment in all of its forms is expensive and increasingly so. The chemical cosh may contain symptoms, but 'cure' or at least amelioration is a labour intensive and thus expensive task. Secondly, the system only 'worked' if the scale of mental impairment was stable. In fact, it has increased exponentially in the last 20 years. Austerity post-2008 has brought the failings of the system into sharp relief. The number of mental health nurses has fallen significantly. Referral rates for mental health services have been rising and waiting times for any form of non-chemical intervention have been lengthening rapidly. It is estimated that at least 25 per cent of the homeless have persistent and long-term mental health issues, while the Prison Reform Trust suggests that 62 per cent of males and 57 per cent of females given custodial sentences (Prison Reform Trust 2015) have some form of mental health problem. Suicide rates are rising amongst the under 30s, and newspapers periodically carry stories about the failings of mental health services. Yet austerity is only one part of the explanation for this picture. A more significant factor has been the corrosion of the responsiveness of the broader welfare system to the needs of those with mental impairments.

If we step back to the last time there was an explosion of mental health issues, in the nineteenth-century, so it becomes possible to view so-called 'modern' issues on a more continuous canvas. In this picture local surveillance, the capacity for local action, retention and processing of stories, the willingness to spend considerable amounts of money and above all an understanding of the complexity of the issues raised by mental impairment and thus the necessity of a complex response, are thrown into very sharp relief. The collapse of modern mental health services is, all other things being equal, inevitable. The nineteenth-century response to the same set of issues provides an unlikely but compelling model for what should happen when they do.

Chapter 6: Thinking Policy

The individual stories of historical figures that pepper this volume and drive its analysis have a modern analogue in evidence given by ordinary people in the coronial court and to enquiries into disability policy and allowances. Above all, we see stories about those with mental, physical and sensory impairment played out time and again in the pages of our national newspapers or through campaigning websites. Considered in the round, these modern stories suggest a policy framework that is failing and a group of policy-makers from across the political spectrum who are out of ideas and out of money. The problem can and will get worse. Obesity, ageing, a rising tide of mental ill-health amongst the young, the inexorable rise of diabetes, and developing antibiotic resistance will all combine to increase the scale of impairment, its intensity and the duration over which impairments have to be lived with and treated. For a country which is already the 'most disabled' in Europe on some indicators, the socio-cultural impact of these trends will be devastating. The impact on the welfare state will be even more so.

Yet this situation is not new. We have, as you will see from the foregoing analysis, been here before in the nineteenth-century. Of course, it cannot be argued that the lessons to be drawn from this period about the way that the State understood and responded to impairments and the way those impairments were constructed into 'disability', are seamlessly transposable to the modern period. On the other hand, and as we have seen here, policy-makers, disability groups and public commentators are rather too apt to define the problems they face as somehow 'modern' and the solutions that they now grapple with as unprecedented. Neither is the case.

Thus, the modern narrative that those with mental, physical and sensory impairments must be enabled (and sometimes forced) into work as both a good in itself and as a way to reduce the poverty that many people with impairments face, was part of the welfare wallpaper in the nineteenth-century. New tests for disability benefits widely defined focus on where someone sits on a spectrum of ability rather than disability. This way of thinking about impairments was central to the relationship between ordinary people and the local State in the nineteenth-century. Indeed, applicants and officials shared a common language of degrees of ability. While the concept of a 'Big Society' has been consigned to the rhetorical dustbin, politicians cannot help themselves but come back again and again to the sense that families and communities could do more for those (notably the aged) with impairments. This sort of partnership was usually at the core of the way that ordinary people in the nineteenth-century were cared for in their communities.

The fact that a rhetorical and strategic infrastructure in relation to impairments is shared across time might seem surprising. Yet it is clear. Our failure to build on this historical knowledge and look for solutions to impending modern crises is also clear. This is unfortunate because as we have shown there is much to learn. Keeping those with impairments out of full and long-term dependency on the State required in the nineteenth-century a dynamic local partnership between the person with the impairment, their variously constructed communities and the welfare system. Officials were often called upon to act quickly and to use welfare payments flexibly in order to support people as they traversed a spectrum of ability and inability. They almost always acted in partnership with families and neighbours, and they carefully calibrated their actions in relation to the current state of ability of claimants. Where those with impairments worked and earned wages, this was not a bar to rapid or significant action by the welfare authorities. Only when someone had confined themselves to bed and thus withdrawn from the public world did the language of disability start to creep in. In this nineteenth-century context, where legal rights to receive relief as opposed to a legal right to apply for it were few, most of those with mental, physical or sensory impairments seem to have retained a moral right to favourable consideration. Local officials familiar with the stories of those who claimed welfare, could and did find it virtually impossible to erase moral rights even if they wanted to in the first place. The legal rights that can so easily be watered down in the face of budget constraints are, arguably, no substitute for the loss of such moral rights over time. Now, as the threat of a new and substantial tide of impairment looms so large, history has very much to teach us.

Bibliography

Primary Sources

Berkshire Record Office D/P 91/8/1, Pangbourne vestry minutes.
Berkshire Record Office D/P 91/18/12, Pangbourne parochial correspondence.
Berkshire Record Office D/P 13918/1-4, Wallingford parochial correspondence.
Bristol Record Office P-StJB-ChW-7-6, St. John the Baptist parochial correspondence.
Bristol Record Office P-StM-OP-5, St. Michael on the Mount Without parochial correspondence.
Hampshire Record Office 25M84/PO55, Lyndhurst vestry minutes.
Manchester Central Library M10/808-815, Hulme letters books.
University of Nottingham Manuscripts and Special Collections, Wr D (Wrench Diaries), 11, 23 and 32.
Northamptonshire Record Office 249p/164-66, Oundle vestry minutes.
Northamptonshire Record Office 249p/216, Oundle letter book.
Northamptonshire Record Office 251p/98-199, Overseers' correspondence, Great Oxendon.
Northamptonshire Record Office 283p/33, Overseers correspondence for Rothersthorpe 1810-1830. See also the parish chest at the parish church.
Northamptonshire Record Office 325p/193 and 194, Thrapston copy letter books.
Northamptonshire Record Office 261p/221-252a, Peterborough overseers' correspondence.
Oxfordshire Record Office MSS. D.D. Par. Rotherfield Greys c.11/1-24, Correspondence and letters.
http://www.prisonreformtrust.org.uk/projectsresearch/mental health.

Secondary Sources

Althammer, B., (ed.), *Bettler in Der Modernen Stadt* (Bern: Peter Lang, 2007).

Andrews, J., Briggs, A., Porter, R., Tucker P. and Waddington K., *The History of Bethlem* (London: Routledge, 1997).

Andrews, J. and Digby, A., (eds), *Sex and Seclusion, Class and Custody: Perspectives on Gender and Class in the History of British and Irish Psychiatry* (Amsterdam: Rodopi, 2004).

Bartley, G., *The Schools for the People: Containing, the History, Development and Present Working of Each Description of English School for the Industrial and Poorer Classes* (London: John Dent, 1871).

Bates, V., '"So Far as I Can Define without a Microscopical Examination": Venereal Disease Diagnosis in English Courts, 1850-1914', *Social History of Medicine*, 26 (2013), 38-55.

Bennett, M., 'Inoculation of the poor against smallpox in eighteenth-century England', in Scott. A., (ed.), *Experiences of Poverty in Late Medieval and Early Modern England and France* (Farnham: Ashgate, 2012), 207-38.

Borsay, A., *Disability and Social Policy in Britain since 1750: A History of Exclusion* (Basingstoke: Palgrave, 2005).

Borsay, A., 'Deaf children and charitable education in Britain 1790–1944', in Borsay, A. and Shapely, P., (eds), *Medicine, Charity and Mutual Aid: The Consumption of Health and Welfare in Britain 1550-1950* (Aldershot: Ashgate, 2007), 71-90.

Borsay, A., 'From representation to experience: Disability in the British advice literature for parents, 1890-1980', in Borsay, A. and Dale, P., (eds) *Disabled Children: Contested Caring, 1850-1979* (London: Pickering and Chatto, 2012), 87-101.

Croley, L., 'A working distinction: Vagrants, beggars, and the labouring poor in mid-Victorian England', *Prose Studies*, 18 (1995), 74-104.

Curtis, J., *An Essay on the Deaf and Dumb* (London: Longman, Rees and Orme, 1829), 68-69.

Davies, A., 'Youth gangs, masculinity and violence in late Victorian Manchester and Salford', *Journal of Social History*, 32 (1998), 349-69.

Delap, L., Griffin, B. and Wills, A., (eds), *The Politics of Domestic Authority in Britain since 1800* (Basingstoke: Palgrave, 2009).

Dyson, R. and King, S., '"The streets are paved with idle beggars": Experiences and perceptions of beggars in nineteenth century Oxford', in Althammer, B., (ed.), *Bettler in Der Modernen Stadt* (Bern: Peter Lang, 2007), 71-102.

Esmail, J., Reading *Victorian Deafness* (Athens: Ohio University Press, 2013).

Ferguson, C., 'The Political Economy of the Street and Its Discontents: Beggars and Pedestrians in Mid-Nineteenth-century London', *Cultural and Social History*, 12 (2015), 27-50.

Garrett, E., Reid, A., Schürer, K. and Szreter, S., *Changing Family Size in England and Wales: Class and Demography in England and Wales, 1891-1911* (Cambridge: Cambridge University Press, 2001).

Gulliver, M., 'Insulting Jean Massieu: Debating Representational Control of Deaf People in Mid-Nineteenth Century Britain', *Social and Cultural History*, 14 (2017), 321-42

Hampton, J., *Disability and the Welfare State in Britain: Changes in Perception and Policy 1948-1979* (Bristol: Policy Press, 2016).

Hennock, E., *The Origin of the Welfare State in England and Germany, 1850-1914: Social Policies Compared* (Cambridge: Cambridge University Press, 2007).

Higgs, E., *Making Sense of the Census: The Manuscript Returns for England and Wales, 1801-1901* (London: Longman, 1989).

Higgs, E., *The Information State in England: The Central Collection of Information on Citizens Since 1500* (Basingstoke: Palgrave, 2004).

Hindle, S., *On the Parish? The Micro Politics of Poor Relief in Rural England 1550-1750* (Oxford: Clarendon Press, 2004).

Hitchcock, T., King, P. and Sharpe, P., (eds), *Chronicling Poverty: The Voices and Strategies of the English Poor, 1640-1840* (Basingstoke: Macmillan, 1997).

Hollen-Lees, L., *The Solidarities of Strangers: The English Poor Laws and the People, 1700-1948* (Cambridge: Cambridge University Press, 1998).

Honeyman, K., *Child Workers in England, 1780-1820: Parish Apprentices and the Making of the Early Industrial Labour Force* (Aldershot: Ashgate, 2007).

Hulonce, L., '"These Valuable Institutions": Educating Blind and Deaf Children in Victorian and Edwardian Swansea', *Welsh History Review*, 27 (2014), 310-37.

Humphries, J., *Childhood and Child Labour in the British Industrial Revolution* (Cambridge: Cambridge University Press, 2010).

Jones, P. and King, S., (eds), *Obligation, Entitlement and Dispute under the English Poor Laws* (Newcastle: Cambridge Scholars Press, 2015).

Jones, P. and King, S., 'From petition to pauper letter: The development of an epistolary form', in Jones, P. and King, S., (eds),

Obligation, Entitlement and Dispute under the English Poor Laws (Newcastle: Cambridge Scholars Press, 2015), 53-77.

King, S., *Poverty and Welfare in England 1700-1850: A Regional Perspective* (Manchester: Manchester University Press, 2000).

King, S. and Timmins, G., *Making Sense of the Industrial Revolution* (Manchester: Manchester University Press, 2001).

King, S., '"Meer pennies for my baskitt": Women, work and the economy of makeshifts in Midland and Northern England, 1700-1840', in Lane, P., Raven, N. and Snell, K. D. M., (eds), *Women, Work and Wages in England, 1600-1850* (Woodbridge: Boydell, 2004), 119-40.

King, S., '"It is impossible for our vestry to judge his case into perfection from here": Managing the distance dimensions of poor relief, 1800-40', *Rural History*, 16 (2005), 161-89.

King, S., Nutt, T. and Tomkins, A., *Narratives of the Poor in Eighteenth Century Britain* (London: Pickering and Chatto, 2006).

King, S., 'Nursing Under the Old Poor Law in Midland and Eastern England 1780-1834', *Journal of the History of Medicine and Allied Sciences*, 69 (2014), 1-35.

King, S., 'Constructing the disabled child in England, 1800-1860', *Family and Community History*, 18 (2015), 56-89.

King, S., 'English pauper letters, 1790s-1830s', *Groniek*, 204/205 (2015b), 305-16.

King, S. and Jones, P., 'Testifying for the poor: Epistolary advocates and the negotiation of parochial relief in England, 1800-1834', *Journal of Social History*, 49 (2016), 351-82.

Lekka, V., *The Neurological Emergence of Epilepsy: The National Hospital for the Paralysed and Epileptic (1870-1895)* (Cham: Springer, 2015).

Lemmings, D. and Walker, C., (eds), *Moral Panics, the Media and the Law in Early Modern England* (Basingstoke: Palgrave, 2009).

Levitan, K., *A Cultural History of the British Census: Envisioning the Multitude in the Nineteenth Century* (Basingstoke: Palgrave, 2011).

Logan, P., *Nerves and Narratives: A Cultural History of Hysteria in Nineteenth-Century British Prose* (Berkeley: University of California Press, 1997).

Mangion, C., '"The business of life": Educating Catholic Deaf Children in Late Nineteenth-Century England', *History of Education*, 41 (2012), 575-94.

Mills, C. and Adderley, P., 'Occupational Exposure to Heavy Metals Poisoning: Scottish Lead Mining', *Social History of Medicine*, 30 (2017), 520-43.

Phillips, G., *The Blind in British Society: Charity, State and Community, c.1780-1930* (Aldershot: Ashgate, 2004).

Philo, C., *A Geographical History of Institutional Provision for the Insane From Medieval Times to the 1860's in England and Wales: This Space Reserved for Insanity* (Lewiston: Edwin Mellen Press, 2004).

Porter, R. and Porter, D., *In sickness and in Health: The British Experience 1650-1850* (London: Fourth Estate, 1988).

Razzell, P., *The Conquest of Smallpox: The Impact of Inoculation on Smallpox Mortality in Eighteenth Century Britain* (Firle: Caliban Books, 1977).

Riley, J., *Sickness, Recovery and Death: A History and Forecast of Ill-Health* (Basingstoke: Macmillan, 1989).

Riley, J., *Sick Not Dead: The Health of British Workingmen During the Mortality Decline* (Baltimore: John's Hopkin University Press, 1997).

Shuttleton, D., *Smallpox and the Literary Imagination 1660-1820* (Cambridge: Cambridge University Press, 2007).

Smith, C., 'Living with Insanity: Narratives of poverty, pauperism and sickness in asylum records 1840-1876', in Gestrich, A., Hurren, E. and King, S., (eds), *Poverty and Sickness in Modern Europe: Narratives of the Sick Poor, 1780-1938* (London: Continuum, 2012), 117-41.

Smith, L., *Lunatic Hospitals in Georgian England, 1750-1830* (London: Routledge, 2007).

Snow, S., *Operations Without Pain: The Practice and Science of Anaesthesia in Victorian Britain* (Basingstoke: Palgrave, 2006).

Sokoll, T., 'Old age in poverty: The record of Essex pauper letters, 1780-1834', in Hitchcock, T., King, S. and Sharpe, P., (eds), *Chronicling Poverty: The Voices and Strategies of the English Poor, 1640-1840* (Basingstoke: Macmillan, 1997), 127-54.

Sokoll, T., 'Negotiating a living: Essex pauper letters from London, 1800-1834', *International Review of Social History*, 8 (2000), 19-46.

Sokoll, T., *Essex Pauper Letters 1731-1837* (Oxford: Oxford University Press, 2001).

Snell, K. D. M., *Parish and Belonging: Community, Identity and Welfare in England and Wales 1700-1950* (Cambridge: Cambridge University Press, 2006).

Stanley, P., *For Fear of Pain: British Surgery, 1790-1850* (Amsterdam: Rodopi, 2003).

Storey, N., *Prisons & Prisoners in Victorian Britain* (Stroud: The History Press, 2010).

Suzuki, A., *Madness at Home: The Psychiatrist, the Patient and the Family in England, 1820-1860* (Los Angeles: University of California Press, 2006).

Taylor, J., *Poverty, Migration and Settlement in the Industrial Revolution: Sojourners' Narratives* (Palo Alto: Stanford University Press, 1989).

Thane, P., *Old Age in English History: Past Experiences, Present Issues* (Oxford: Oxford University Press, 2000).

Tomkins, A., 'Workhouse Medical Care from Working-Class Autobiographies, 1750-1834', in Reinarz, J. and Schwarz, L., (eds), *Medicine and the Workhouse* (Rochester: University of Rochester Press, 2013), 86-102.

Turner, D., *Disability in Eighteenth-Century England: Imagining Physical Impairment* (London: Routledge, 2012).

Williams, G., *Angel of Death: The Story of Smallpox* (Basingstoke: Palgrave, 2011).

Wilson, A., 'Midwifery in the "medical marketplace"', in Jenner, M. and Wallis, P., (eds), *Medicine and the Market in England and its Colonies, c.1450-c.1850* (Basingstoke: Palgrave, 2007), 153-74